# Seasons of Poetry from the Tree of Life

PAULA JEAN HIGHT-SULLINS

authorHOUSE®

AuthorHouse™
1663 Liberty Drive
Bloomington, IN 47403
www.authorhouse.com
Phone: 1-800-839-8640

Published by AuthorHouse    05/02/2013

ISBN: 978-1-4817-3301-4 (sc)
ISBN: 978-1-4817-3300-7 (hc)
ISBN: 978-1-4817-3299-4 (e)

Library of Congress Control Number: 2013905307

# DEDICATION

I wish to dedicate this book to my parents, children, grandchildren, relatives, and friends who have been inspirations for my poetry.

# CONTENTS

# Fall

# Winter

# Acknowledgments

Ginger Mullenix for editing my books

Ginger and Paula

# Spring

# Haiku: Spring in the Meadow

Spring in the meadow

Clear water trickles and flows

Farm fresh and glowing

# Sudden Shower

Sitting comfortably in the old, steel, lawn chair on the covered patio, I yawn as I look skyward and see clouds filling the sky with a grey, oyster colored canopy. A few light mists of rain spew as they fall intermittently, and for a while, the tepid temperatures make it a pleasant repose. I close my eyes and listen to the whistles and chatter of the birds as they fly branch to branch as a gentle breeze blows.

The whirring sound of an automobile driving past temporarily overtakes all the other sounds. Then I hear the cocky, old, rooster crow from his perch and another in the distance echoes his call. I relax in this natural bliss until I jump, when the booming roll of thunder resonates in, around, and through.

Soon the strong, rhythmic, patter of the rain hitting the green, fiber glass roof upsets my relaxed state. When the wind gusts and the blowing rain cause a hasty retreat to the dry safety inside my home. I watch for a while as the rain falls and hits the window panes, but when the thunder rolls and the lightning flashes, I promptly close the blinds on natures increasingly turbulent scene.

*Paula Jean Hight-Sullins*

# My Favorite Treat

Hey, I'll bet you can't guess my favorite edible treat?

Candy? Ice cream? No, for me a sour pickle can't be beat.

My mouth waters and they beckon me as I step inside the door.

I can't resist when I see them in a jar on the counter at the store.

So plump and juicy, I anticipate the taste as I ring the service bell.

I smile as he unscrews the lid and that delicious aroma I smell.

I quickly give him the money and he hands me a jumbo green delight.

I say thank you and sit on the store bench and relish every sour bite.

Mom says, "I've never seen anyone love a sour pickle as much as you.

You could eat pickles and nothing else, but why you like them so, I haven't a clue."

My brother says "I know why. It's 'cause you're pickle crazy" and tries to steal it just to start a fuss.

Daddy says, "I don't care how many you eat, you're still my sweet little 'Pickle Puss.'"

I don't know why anyone bothers to comment 'cause I don't care what they may say,

Just as long as I can have a big, green, juicy, sour pickle at last once every day.

# Oh, My Poor Baby

Oh, my poor baby, do you have the flu?

You sound just terrible, what can I do?

Here, let me fluff your pillow, straighten your sheets, and the curtains I'll draw.

I'll make some chicken noodle soup and bring ginger ale in a glass with a straw.

Let me massage your shoulders and back. I know how achy you must feel.

Now, you just relax, while I decide what to fix you for your next meal.

Bless your heart; you're so stopped up and stuffy in your head.

Let me rub some Menthelatum on your chest and, put the tissues by your bed

Hold this under your tongue. Oh my, your fever has hit 103.

Here's a wet cloth for your forehead and take two of these for me.

It's amazing how a six foot two, one hundred eighty pound man turns into a child of three

When the miseries of the flu bug stops him in his tracks, and brings him to his knee.

*Paula Jean Hight-Sullins*

Ewe!

Who?

Me?

You?

No?

Flo?

Oh?

So?

Sue?

Too?

New?

Blue?

Ewe!

# The Grapevine

O. K. What's happening? Spill it. Tell me. Who's in the poop?

Nothing escapes you. You know everything, so give the scoop.

Who's sleeping and slipping around on who?

What's the latest scandal and what did they do?

REEEaaally, oh my, that's so raucous and bold!

Ha, Ha. He did? I'll bet he never wanted that told.

So she's pregnant not fat and she's not too sure by whom?

Her ex pays child support for six; one more could spell his doom

What? They just married last month and now she's left and gone away.

'Cause he's sleeping with her sister, oh, my, I don't know what to say!

And another wedding is in the planning stage for "Gad About" Bre.

First there was the accountant, then lawyer and this will be number three.

You say the wedding will be the biggest, most lavish, gala event of the season

And it will happen soon because squelching the rumors that he's gay is the reason!

Oh dear, are you very sure that's all you have to report today?

Talking to you is so enlightening; you've always so much to say.

Me? Well, let's see, I'm not pregnant, my divorce was years ago and I'm not gay, a bitch, or a gay bitch.

I've a fantastic family, my home is a colonial mansion, and my investments have made me filthy rich.

How about you? Have you been well? Is there anyone or anything new?

You're cruising to Bali and then jetting to Spain for something to do.

No, I wish I could go with you, but I have that charity thing to do.

But I know you'll have loads of fun and plenty to report the next time I see you.

Hugs and kisses my dear—it's always so lovely visiting with you

Ta, Ta, now and remember to speak kindly of me, 'Cause I'm kin to you.

# I'm Just Sayin'

For many years now I have searched for the right man for me and I thought I would know when we kissed

I have pondered why I haven't found him yet, and I'll tell you, that I have decided that the man I seek does not exist

I do know exactly what I am looking for is a combination of traits in my ideal, perfect man's profile

Cute, smart, witty, ethical, brave, empathetic, loyal, loving and moral with both feet planted firmly on the ground all the while

At one time, I thought I had found one, but he soon turned out to be a big lout

And I found out through this experience exactly what I didn't want and what my quest was all about

Where are all the real men? What happened to them?

I want a man blended with the traits of John Wayne, Pat Boone, and Elvis rolled into one super brute

I have looked and looked for at least twenty years and have not found one. Where is the big galoot?

If you should find one, hold on and don't let him go

Then call me immediately and let me know

*Paula Jean Hight-Sullins*

We'll need to clone him, 'cause from my research he just might be the last real man in existence

And losing him would be tragic; we need more like him to give others like me a chance.

But until then, I'll keep on looking and praying

That's all I can do . . . . I'm just sayin'.

# Love is What You Do, Not What You Say.

Love is what you do, not what you say.

You can say, I love you, about anything all day.

I love your dress, I love your hair,

I love your smile, I love your shoes. Is that a new pair?

Jesus said, "I love you", but he didn't stop there.

He stretched out his arms and died and showed the depth of his care.

Real love is not a feeling, for those can change with the wind.

It is commitment and actions that show you are true blue to the end.

Love is not what you say; it's what you do.

So say it, but then show it with follow through.

*Paula Jean Hight-Sullins*

# Hey Ho Daddy-O

Hey ho daddy-o
Let's bop and swing
And go, go, go

Rock and roll
Feel the beat
Baby you got soul

One for the money and two for the show
Got my dancing shoes on
Let's go, go, go

Do the hand jive, moving on up and back
Playing nick, nack, patty, wack
Sounding like a train on the railroad track.

Now if you got the money honey, I got the time
All dressed to the nines as we stroll down the line
Stuck on you like glue as long as it's on your dime.

Mix it up with the shimmy, shimmy shake
Shimmy, shimmy, cocoa-puffs
Pour it up, stir it up, and let it bake

Sugar shack and blueberry hill
Twist on up and locomotion back
The beat won't let my feet stay still

Sunshine, rainbows, and lollypops
I got the rock and roll fever
And the beat never stops

Nine, ten, eleven o'clock rock
When I'm into the beat
I don't need no clock

The rhythm's got my feet to move
Keeping time to the music
Hey ho daddy-o I'm in the groove

# A New Place to Throw Down

There's a new restaurant in town.

It's the "in" place to throw down.

I'm dying to go, but I hate to go alone.

My son is busy, and my friend is cruising, so I'm on my own.

I even called my sister who resides with her family in the next town.

I asked her to come visit and said we'd go out to eat when she came down.

She declined as usual because she has four kids and they keep her busy.

Between her work, picking up kids, and letting them off, she makes me dizzy.

So, I resigned that I wouldn't go, until my curiosity finally got the best of me and I decided to go alone and try to have fun.

When I got there the place was packed and I was seated at a cozy little table for one.

I sat there smiling and soaking in the beautiful decoration and atmosphere for a while.

Then the waiter brought the menu and as I looked, I could no longer smile.

Even the soup was $12.99 and the salad was an additional $8.95

And, unfortunately I was so hungry that with that little lunch I could barely survive.

I thought about it and decided I would add another charge to my overworked credit card.

I searched the menu searching for a filling meal that was cheap, and I looked really hard.

I finally found a ground steak and tater plate for $14.00 and I thanked the Lord.

It took a while, but when it arrived, it tasted great and I ate it like it was a filet mignon.

It melted in my mouth and I vowed to myself to return as soon as they printed a 20% off coupon.

I don't know why I was so hesitant 'cause now I was so glad that I braved it alone,

And as soon as I got home, I called all my friends and bragged about the restaurant on the phone.

# Ain't Got No Money Blues

Ain't got no money

Cain't buy no shoes

Ain't got no money

For clothes, food or dues

Ain't got no money,

Cain't even buy gas to go to the sto'

Ain't got no money

The rent man's knocking at my do'.

Ain't got no money, don' know what to do

Ain't got no money, I got the po' man blues.

# Why Should I?

Change what? Why should I? What's in it for me?
I never heard such, who gave you the authority?

You don't know me, you don't understand.
I know what I'm doing, man.

You're not my boss, my parent or significant other.
You're not my aunt, uncle, sister, or brother.

Just leave me alone, just let me be, and it'll be O.K.
'Cause if you try to force me, I'll make your day.

But you won't like it, 'cause it won't stop with what I say.
Learn this. I do things in my on time and in my own way!

So, if you want me to do a good job and make you smile,
Then back off, leave me alone, and it'll be worth your while.

# What's Wrong?

I think I'm "kinda" smart and classy, not a dork, but I know my stuff.

Sometimes I feel dumb and different, so in order to fit in I have to act tough.

Though I'm kind of popular and accepted by a few of the kids at school, I have to ask; am I crazy?

Is something wrong with me? Or is something wrong with the other kids in society?

The so called "cool" kids used to call me names and it made me feel strange and have self doubt.

I want to be "cool" but, I'm taunted and torn because they say to act like them and "fit in or get out".

I was raised as a Christian with morals and values, but when I act accordingly I'm told that I'm acting like a loser.

So, to have a "cool" image and fit in, I have to act like them, which is like a user, smoker, and a boozer.

I can't tell my parents 'cause they have no clue; they think I act the same at home as I do at school.

Most of these kids are from "juvey" and I'm scared sometimes, but I dare not act like a nerd or a fool.

What with the gangs, Nazi's, emotionally disturbed, and those who are a drama or drag queen,

I'm scared someone will pull a knife or gun on me just for the "coolness" of being mean.

I keep my cell phone handy just in case I have to call someone for help or dial 911.

Sometimes I've been so paranoid and scared, I've thought of buying a gun.

But even the illegal ones are expensive and I don't have the cash right now,

And even if I could buy one, I don't know if I could use one anyhow.

While I'm young, I want to be happy. I hate this! I'm not being me.

I need acceptance and security in order to feel free so I can really be me.

I pray from my heart to God's every day and night.

Please keep me alive and make my future safe and bright.

# What Will You Be?

What will you grow up to be my precious granddaughter dear?

Will you marry, have children and live close, or far away from here?

I know you would make an excellent mother and wife.

But you are so smart and talented, you could do so many things in your life

I can see you now taking the oath of office for the presidency, standing hand over heart, as the American flag is unfurled.

Or, with cameras rolling, accepting the Nobel Prize for finding a cure for cancer or bringing peace to the world.

You could even lead the first mission to Mars,

Going where no one has gone before, traveling among the stars

There are so many things you could do and be

The world is full of fantastic opportunity

You could be an actress accepting an Oscar in your haute couture jewels and gown

And mentioning me as you clutch the golden trophy as flashbulbs flash all around

Let's see, a brain surgeon, accountant, super model, lawyer, or Cordon Bleu chef

So many ways that you could go, just promise me to think it through and decide for yourself.

Because working can be a boring, dreaded chore, please listen to me as someone who knows.

Do something you enjoy and your enthusiasm and satisfaction throughout the years grows

So, whatever you do Madame President, Your Excellency, the Honorable Doctor Dear

I will be proud and support you and be there for you if you need me as long as I am here.

# On Mother's Day

What can I do, or say, to express my love and gratitude to you on Mother's Day?

You have filled my life with your love and care; and I can count on you to always be there,

You have been my teacher, my role model, and my friend;

You keep me going when I want to give up, or give in.

You are my conscience, my advocate, and spiritual guide;

From you there is nothing that I can hide.

From the bottom of my heart, I want to thank you.

So, "Thanks" Mom for everything, and for just being you!

# I No Longer Cry on Mother's Day

I no longer cry when you don't call or visit me on my birthday or Mother's day, for I have already cried too many tears.
Though it still boggles my mind as to why this is. I might understand if you had suffered any abuse or neglect through the years.

But your life was full of the best I could offer; you never missed out on anything, and most would say you had a blessed life.
I was there for you through thick and thin times, through ups and downs, supporting, nurturing or picking up the pieces through all the strife.

Yet, you treat me as if I do not exist. Why? I was always your cheerleader and advocate, choosing to see the best in you and your potential.
In repayment for this you have lied to me, slandered me, ignored me and treated strangers and acquaintances with more respect than I, and as if they were more important and special.

Don't you miss me? Don't you have any fond memories? I am getting old now and you still remain silent. Why? I want to understand. All I want to know is why? Can your heart be so cold? Didn't you appreciate the sacrifices I made, or the love and care I gave? Will you even come to my bedside or my funeral when I die?

I have thought long and hard and sent many prayers trying to understand. Are you trying to punish me? What did I do? I want the truth but never get it. You used to be such a loving child. What happened to you?

Many days and nights I have agonized over these questions because I really want to understand and I think that if I knew, I could make things better, because isn't that what Mother's do?

*Paula Jean Hight-Sullins*

You are not the same little boy I raised to be a good, respectful son. You were attentive, loving, and thoughtful then.

You were such a good child, I miss that child I knew. I just don't know what happened to you or when.

# Summer

# Summertime Fun

Warm summer breezes blow the aroma of burgers and weenies cooking on the grill.

Water splashes and hits my glasses and face as kids play in the pool.

A domino game is in full force at the card table on the far side of the shaded yard.

Aunt's, grannies, nieces, daughters, granddaughters, and friends chat happily as they set the picnic table and come and go from the kitchen.

Aunt Sally, Uncle Fudge and Great Uncle Joe finally arrive as he pulls his oxygen along behind.

It's the annual family reunion that I always dread preparing for but, for which I am always glad and enjoy, once I'm there with my kith and kin.

# Vacation

Skimming the deep

Smoothly sailing along

Making memories we'll keep

No work, no worry, no care

Going and doing what we want

Relaxing in the tropical air

The wind blows constantly

Fully billowing the sail

Light fluffy clouds in the sky

Look like a baby Beluga whale

Our coastal vacation is in full swing

Enjoying all of the ocean's delights

With no worries nor wants for anything.

# Texas Heat

In the Texas heat, if you're not out and about at seven

You'll surely fry your hide if you're out at eleven.

Some people think that lots and lots of heat is neat.

Not me, I stay cool sitting in front of the AC vent in my recliner seat.

Texas heat is great for frogs, snakes, scorpions, and lizards

But fair skinned people better stay inside or they'll fry their own gizzards.

# 110 Degrees in the Shade

It's been so hot lately it makes me swoon
Hot at night, in the morning, and at noon
I can't believe it's only June

I guess the snakes and lizards like this weather O.K.
And the weatherman and my thermometer say
There'll be triple digit temperatures now every day

Just walking into the yard to get my paper makes sweat pour down
It gets in my mouth and stings my eyes, and I feel like I am going to drown
I look for clouds and pray that rain will soon fall on this parched ground

But even when we get a few drops, we can't breathe 'cause the humidity
makes the air steamy hot and heavy all around.
We wear short shorts and sleeveless shirts, turn down the air, and close
the blinds and pull all the shades down
Oh, what I wouldn't give for some good old wintertime snow and ice on
the ground

Everyday its gets hotter and this record heat has kept my electric bill soaring,
Eggs don't fry on the sidewalk, they burn to a crisp, not just outside, but
on regular flooring
That's why I stay inside watching reruns on TV though it's mind
numbing and boring,

I go out by the light of the moon, which for me is a very big switch.
So, now the neighbors all think I am some kind of lunatic or witch
Especially 'cause I contort and dance when the 'skeeters' bite and make
me itch

*Paula Jean Hight-Sullins*

Every day the weatherman says tomorrow and the rest of the week will be scorchers and that's all
So I go in and make me a glass of lemonade in an icy cold glass that is tall
I sure do hope and pray that I can survive until the cooler weather in the fall

# You Did It—You Passed

Let me shake your hand. I'm so very proud of you son.

You passed your driving test and even said it was fun.

Now to show you how proud I am there's something special I'm going to do.

I am so happy with your new driving skills, I have a surprise gift for you.

Let's walk outside. Now, close your eyes and I'll lead.

I've got something for you that all Texas boys need.

Careful now . . . . O.k. Open your eyes. What do you see?

*It's a pickup! Is it really for me?*

Yes, it is, but with it comes responsibility.

It's a 1985 Ford, as sturdy as can be.

Now son, it needs a little sprucing up,

But it runs smooth and there's even a holder for your cup.

*Well, Pop, you just leave the sprucing up to me.*

*Is the engine a 4/6/ or 8 cylinder? And are these dual tailpipes, I see?*

Yes, indeed. It's eight cylinders. Let's go for a spin. Here's the key.

*Yes! Yee Haw! This is just the greatest, dad.*

*I honestly think this is the best gift I've ever had.*

The air conditioner doesn't work, but the heater works great.

It's a little rusty and you have to kick it to open the tailgate.

*Oh, well, it does run pretty good, and now that we've taken a few spins,*

*If it's O.K., I'm going to take it over and show it to all of my friends.*

Sure son, I'm glad you like your new ride.

I'm proud of you and my heart swells with pride.

*Oh, Dad, I'm so happy, I've already got big plans for my new ride.*

*I am going to buy new seat covers and paint some flames on the side.*

*I love it so. Thank you. I promise to take care of it you'll see.*

*I'm going fix her up and I think I'll name her Bettie.*

*Just thinking about it brings me happiness and joy.*

*'Cause nothing can come between a pickup and a Texas cowboy.*

# Do You Know How Special You Are?

When we are in a crowd, you are the only one I see
My feelings for you run deep and I tingle from deep inside of me

Even after all the hurt and heartache I've been through,
You make me trust and believe in love again, with all that you do

Your kisses ignite my heart with abiding love and passion so deep.
I resign to you alone, and promise all my love forever to keep.

*Paula Jean Hight-Sullins*

# Well, Look Who's Here

Well, my goodness, would you look who's here?

Hello there. It's been quite awhile my dear.

In fact, I think it was our last date on the fourth of July.

We were at the lake watching the fireworks explode in the sky.

Long time, no see. So, how are you?

You look nice. Tell me, what's new?

*It's good to see you and reminisce, but I came with a purpose, too.*

*I'm getting married, you see, and I came especially to invite you.*

*We're getting married at my friend's antebellum home*

*Then for our honeymoon, we are flying to Rome.*

*I met her in July and immediately the love sparks flew.*

*I've never met anyone as wonderful as her, just one look and I knew.*

*She's so tiny and petite, but strong 'cause she works out and has muscles from her head to her feet.*

*She's a real dynamo, irreplaceable at her job and super girl at home. She's just so neat!*

*We were such good friends, I just had to let you know.*

Uh huh, good friends, well, of course, I should know.

Sooo, you met her in July after our date and the fireworks show?

*Well, yes. Our wedding will be special and you're such a good friend, I do hope you can go.*

*You know it will be a really grand affair.*

*Be sure to wear your best evening wear.*

It sounds divine, just *too* perfect for you two.

But . . . . *my good friend* . . . . I have already made plans with my someone new.

So, I must say to you and your bride, lots of luck . . . . and now, fare the well.

. . . . And before you go, there's just one more thing . . . . my good friend . . . as far as I'm concerned . . . . well . . .

. . . .You and your Miss Perfect can just go straight to_____!

# Bad News Travels Faster and Farther

Isn't it strange how bad news travels faster and farther than good news.

My son and his wife had a baby two years ago and he's still precious even though he is now in his "terrible twos".

The announcement was in the paper and I posted pictures to Facebook of all different angles and views.

Well, yesterday, I went to lunch with my second cousin whose been a fairly close friend.

I just had to show her my grandson's newest pictures, especially the one showing the dimple in his chin.

And she looked at me in shock and said, "I didn't know you were a grandmother!"

*I said, "Why yes, he just turned two yesterday and we are now expecting another".*

We continued to chat and as the conversation and stories continued to unfold,

She shook her head and said, "Well, I hate to say anything, but I feel you must be told".

"How unfortunate it is about our cousin's sixteen year old son.

It seems that he stole his parent's new car just for fun.

He crashed it at the grocery store and is now wanted and on the run".

My mouth flew open in disbelief and shock.

After all, I thought we were all of good stock.

I'm telling you, she was a fountain of knowledge and told me all the latest scandals and news.

Complete with the details and of course her "unbiased" views.

Well, the minute I got home I called my cousin to offer support.

She laughed and asked who gave me such an erroneous report.

*I said, "You know, even if it was a relative, I would never divulge my source*

*But did any of this really happen? I am curious of course."*

"Well, yes and no" she said. "Let me tell you how it really went down."

"You see I went to lunch and a movie with my friend Jane Scott, and since she lives on the far side of town,

I met her halfway, parked my car, and left it on the bank parking lot.

The day before, I had promised to drive my son to his basketball game, but I totally forgot.

I guess I was looking forward to the movie where it is cool and I could relax and escape this scorching hot.

My son's a good boy and he called me, but we were at the movies, and my phone was on mute.

So he called his dad, but he was too busy to talk as he was with a customer with spending loot.

*Paula Jean Hight-Sullins*

He went home and after he read the note I had left for his dad, he took the extra key and walked to the bank, got my car, and drove to the game."

*"Sounds normal to me and, I have to say, if it had been me, I would have done the same."*

"But, when we returned, my car was gone. Stolen, I thought, so I called the police and they issued a warrant, you see.

I never thought about him, because of my conclusion jumping brain, there is no one else to blame, but me!

Later that night when my son returned from the game,

He decided to park the car back at the place from whence it came.

When he pulled in, the sirens and lights started to wail and flash.

It spooked him so much that instead of the brake, he stomped on the gas and drove through the super market front window glass.

Then the police arrested my startled son, handcuffed him, and took him in to jail.

Of course when the real story finally came out, he was released without having to pay bail.

Isn't it amazing how people latch onto the bad.

It's an ironic end to the awful week that we had.

She could have reported the Eagle Scout honor and medal my son received last week.

I guess she wouldn't though because her son is so mousey and meek.

I suppose she is jealous and just wanted my son to look bad,

Especially because that is the highest honor any of our troop has ever had".

"I am so glad I called," I said really relieved.

"People rush to tell the bad things and I'm so gullible I really believed.

But, I guarantee that if there is a next time, I will proudly share the good news of his Eagle Scout Distinction,

And every bad thing I hear, I will counter with something good, and hopefully cause what was meant for bad to suffer extinction".

# Are We Having Fun Yet?

Have you noticed that only young people and old people fraternize?

Seems the middle-aged working class has no real time to socialize

When you are young the goal is to greet, meet, date and mate

When you retire, you greet, meet, seat, eat, and retreat

When you have a family or a career or both, you no longer have extra time

You have projects and deadlines and you have to change your plans on a dime

There are practices, games, dance rehearsals, committees, or business conferences that leave no time for anything more than pleasant greetings.

And though everyone seems amiable, time for real socializing takes a scheduled meeting.

Of course there's Facebook where you "socialize" by reading up and commenting on what your relatives and friends are doing or have done

You check out the newest pictures posted and it looks like they are going to exciting places and having so much fun

So not to be out done you take a short trip with your kids to visit the zoo

And you take lots of pictures of everything you and your crew do

All of you are laughing, smiling and having fun

And you post it to Facebook as soon as you're done

Then back into the daily, hectic routine you delve.

And you eat your sandwich alone at your desk at twelve.

Cause taking one little jaunt with the kids has made you behind a whole week.

The trip was fun but you want someone to tell. Someone to chat with as you share your lunch is whom you seek.

You look at the young adults who look so energetic and happy as they hang out in groups around town.

You look at the retirees as groups board buses for bingo, ships to cruise, or play canasta at each other's houses and all around.

What happened to one on one friend communication, camaraderie and just having fun?

Surely there is a way to have it all. I'll just finish this work and think about that when I'm done.

*Paula Jean Hight-Sullins*

# Shopping

Oh, rats! No eggs, milk, or cereal for my breakfast today.

I guess I'll have to go to the grocery store even though it is out of my way.

I could borrow some milk and cereal from my neighbor next door

But she loves to talk and by the time I did that I could have been finished at the store.

I'll make a list and it won't take long and I'll be in and out.

I know where everything is located so I'll just quickly maneuver about.

Then I'll breeze through the self checkout and I'll be on my way.

Now let's see the first item on my list is margarine, so I'll start at the back of the store.

Look at that, the eggs are on sale, I could save a dollar or more.

I'll buy two dozen. Hmmm . . . . my sister will want some, I'll make it one more.

Oh yes, I also need dish soap, laundry powder, and cheese.

Done and done; yes I'd like to taste a sample of these.

Mmmm . . . . these are delicious. I'll take four of these please.

Now where is that list? I must have dropped it somewhere in the store?

Let's see, I think I've gotten everything; I can't think of anymore.

O.k. In and out quickly . . . . and it's time to go

Self checkout—zip, zip, zip—pay. I love it so!

Then hurry home to unload, and put away.

Now for a little cereal and restart my day.

Oh, no! I forgot the milk when I was at the store.

I don't have the time to go back, so . . . . I guess . . . .

I'll borrow some from my neighbor next door.

# Memorial Day

I wave the flag as the uniformed men and women parade by me.
They are veterans, young and old, who fought so we could live free.

My heartbeat quickens and swells with pride,
As tears fall to my cheeks for those who have died.

Nameless soldiers sacrificing themselves for me and you,
Paying the ultimate price for the Red, White, and Blue.

We pay homage to these American heroes as one nation under God,
united, and free;
Remembering these brave patriots and their battles to preserve our
liberty.

Giving us a future where no tyranny or torture makes us hide.
Where we live without fear in a land where hope and opportunity abide.

With heartfelt thanks for these brave and honorable men we humbly pray,
And, we commemorate their unselfish service this Memorial Day.

# One Nation Under God

Our nation without God will crumble and fall.
There will be no happiness and no freedom for all.

There will be selfishness, dishonor, and greed.
For without God there will be pestilence and need.

Open your eyes, minds, and hearts today.
Let us see that one nation under God is the only way.

Our success has always been tethered in God's grace.
Without His guidance and blessing a bleak future we face.

Let us repent of our errant ways, kneel and humbly pray.
Dear God, forgive our sins and bless this nation today.

For we cannot succeed if we continue on this ungodly path we trod.
So, please listen, we must fall on our knees and give this nation back to God.

*Paula Jean Hight-Sullins*

# Fall

# I Love the Color Red

You know what? I love the color red.

I have red curtains and a red bedspread.

Some say they see red when they are angry

But that is not what red means to me.

Red is vibrant as well as exciting.

To me it is happiness and very inviting.

Red is the color of my favorite pair of boots.

It is the color of apples, one of my favorite fruits.

And, it is the color of Jesus blood that he shed for me.

So really how could red stand for anything bad or being angry?

I love it and I don't care if red is what I see,

'cause red is the very best color to me.

# Hooray! A Package is at My Front Door

Hooray! A package is sitting on the porch at my front door

"It's the book I ordered," I say happily as I rip open the box sitting on the floor

How wonderful to open a box and get a new book

I have to sniff it and hold it and flip the pages to take a look

And I read every word on the back and end flaps, too

Then sit back and as I read, I meet and get acquainted with the characters and what they do

Some may be old friends I've met in previous editions, or completely new

I might read a few chapters, or the whole book before I'm through

Learning as I read about castles, knights, ladies and kings

And famous or infamous people, doing incredible or crazy things

They may be inventing something amazing and new, or trying to fly on homemade wings

I might learn how to bake a rhubarb pie or how to batter and bake onion rings

I know that E-books are the latest rage and are making the news

*Paula Jean Hight-Sullins*

They are great, and you can carry a whole library of books from which to choose

But you can't feel, touch or smell an e-book, for a book is much more than the printed word

Thinking of doing away with the physical book, gives me the blues and though I might be considered a nerd

E-books are nice, but if I had to choose only one, I'd choose a hardback book to see, touch, smell, or even hug

Books are my friends and much more fun; so please do not take hard copy books away

Because they are the best and I'd choose them over e-books any day

# Time Passes Quickly

Time passes so quickly and it has been said

That one day you are born, and a week later you're dead

I lived each day of my life without ever thinking,

About how our life clock will eventually stop ticking.

From the time we take our first breath our clock starts ticking away the seconds, minutes, hours and days.

I admit that I was so busy performing the necessary rituals of life and doing things my way

That I have lost some precious moments that I will never get back.

But there are times I have taken notice and when I remember, they are vivid and nothing lack

Some of those times are extremely happy, some are sad, and some bittersweet, but all I've savored.

I wish that now as I enter old age, I could go back and revisit some of the days I missed and times that I wavered.

But all I can do now is remember, and respectfully remind those who are younger to slow down and enjoy the time

Because the clock ticks steadily without missing a beat and it does not run backwards for us to replay what we missed in our prime.

*Paula Jean Hight-Sullins*

So take time to spend time with those you love, those that mean the most, for time, though steady, seems to fly

Make notes in your mind of all you observe, feel, and experience and be diligent to not let the really important things in your life pass you by.

# I Love Football, Don't you?

Sorry, I can't go with you because I've got to be at home at two.

I've got to see what my favorite football team is gon'na do.

There's the kick off and it got a real good bounce.

The boys look good and are ready to pounce.

First down, through the fourth and the opponent only gained eight yards.

The boys are doing great; I love watching those defensive guards.

Now in comes our "A-1" quarterback to the helm

A flag already? False start, what's wrong with them?

Try again. Good snap, but where's the quarterback's protection? He's sacked and down.

What's going on? Which one of you tripped and let our quarterback hit the ground?

He's getting up slow, I hope he's not hurt.

O.K. third down-time to show your stuff and make them eat dirt.

OH, NOOooo . . . . Are you color blind? You threw it to the black shirt not the blue shirted guy!

*Paula Jean Hight-Sullins*

I guess that sack addled you for a while we're lucky he fumbled now you can give it another try.

It's too far for a field goal, we've got to go for it and make a long pass.

Oh, what did you do? It was way over his head and just bounced on the grass.

Here comes our defensive line. Now stay with them, don't let them gain an inch, it's your turn

Show them your stuff and make them go down in flames and burn.

How could you let them get that far? They're within field goal range!

Did you guys sleep instead of going to practice? You are really playing strange.

Now, Mr. Quarterback, please listen to my advice

Just take it easy and make your throws precise.

That's all we ask of you and nothing more.

Now let's see if we can't advance and score.

That's the way! Just take your time, look down the field, pick out your man, and . . . .

What? How can that be? He never misses. Does he need super glue on his hands?

Those guys need intense two a day practices or more.

If they can't do better; they need to be shown the door.

This is a travesty. The crowd is moaning and booing from the stands.

What a relief, it's half time, hopefully they'll get it together while listening to the bands.

Here we go again, 1$^{st}$ down, no gain. 2$^{nd}$ down the same,

A perfect spiral and a beautiful catch. Now that's how you play the game!

It's been tit for tat since halftime and now comes the kicker. O.K. little guy, it's all up to you.

The players line up, the ball is snapped, and the kick is perfect, but the coach called a timeout.

What is he thinking? This means that we have to kick again and the point didn't count.

But, I know he can do it, there he goes and he's kicked the ball.

Oh, no! The kick is too short! The other team has won it all!

That imbecile coach lost this game with his timeout.

Why'd he do it? They ought'a fire him; he's such a lout!

Now, who do they play next Sunday at two?

I know I'll be watching 'cause I love football. Don't you?

*Paula Jean Hight-Sullins*

# I Do! Do You?

You know what? I want to be a millionaire.

Don't you? Being poor is just so unfair!

I've worked every day since I was a teen.

Graduated, married and had a family in between.

The time I spent toiling away was to buy food and pay the rent.

Looking back now, I should've saved every penny and lived in a tent.

'Cause that's the only way I can see that I could have become a millionaire.

And if I had, today I'd be living the good life without a worry or care

I would be generous, too! All my relatives would get new houses and Cadillac's.

I'd give to the poor so they would have food and warm clothes on their backs.

So, why oh why can't I be a millionaire?

I'd be such a good one; it just isn't fair!

Maybe I could go on a game show on T.V.

Invent a new product, or win the lottery.

I guess that seems a little far-fetched at this stage of the game.

I really wish that Trump, Winfrey, or Rockefeller was my name.

I really want to be a millionaire with homes all over and a private jet.

Maybe if I pawn all my stuff; how much do you think I could get?

I want to live the rest of my life eating bonbons by the pool without a worry or care.

'Cause dang it, I really deserve to be a millionaire!

*Paula Jean Hight-Sullins*

# I Could Lose a Few Pounds

I thought as I tried on some pants and looked in the store mirror, "I could lose a few pounds."

It's been a few years, but I was an athlete in high school so I'll just walk it off. It'll only take a few rounds.

I live on a circle so as soon as I got home I put on my running shoes and energetically started around.

The first time I made it just fine, but the second time I made it only because I was chased by a hound.

The third time, I decided to slow up my pace, but I only made it halfway round and I had to sit on the ground.

I was gasping for air and after I finally caught my breath, I tried to get up, but fell back down.

Angry with myself, I gathered all that I had left of my stamina and grit.

And I tried again, but alas all my energy was spent and I just couldn't do it.

I sat a while, putting off the inevitable as long as I could, hoping I would revive, but I didn't, so I called my husband on the cell phone to come get me.

He was happy to do so, as usual, and he replied with concern, "What the hell! You're where? Sitting under which tree?"

Then when he got there, he had to carry me to the car and then to my bed.

My body was aching with pain from the tip of my toes to the top of my head.

I made him rub me all over with Deep Heat

And then massage my tootsies, he's so sweet.

Then I turned on the heating pad and took the last pain pill the dentist had prescribed.

I don't drink, but if I would have had some whiskey I would have definitely imbibed.

The pain pills kicked in and I went soundly to sleep and didn't wake until dawn.

That's when I made a new plan and it is that these few pounds are staying on!

# Pleasingly Plump

It is always hard for me to lose weight, cause my metabolism is slow, and I kinda' like to eat,

I have been told this extra weight makes me pleasingly plump which fits me cause I'm so sweet.

But I am running out of big clothes to wear and most of my buttons and zippers won't meet.

I am single so I want to be thin to meet a nice man to marry, but I'm afraid, I just can't compete.

My skinny friend said, "Just do what I do and drink yourself thin. It's so easy. You must try the liquid diet".

And it did sound easy so, I picked up a pack at the discount store and with resolve I decided to try it.

I took my vitamins and tried to drink that chocolate stuff. I did it for a week, and I guess that I am the only person who gained weight on it.

Seems everything that passes through my lips always ends up around my waist and hips. I guess, I'll have to have my jaw wired shut and just stay at home and knit.

The first day I tried to just go with bread and water and I did so very well that when I weighed, I had lost one and a half pounds.

I thought that I would do another day to really get this thing under way and when I weighed I had lost another pound. I was really covering ground.

But the third day, hump day, I had to eat, so I went with my friend and got a sandwich at the cafe.

I told her of my weighty plight and bragged about how good I'd been doing by losing those three pounds as we drove on our way.

The sandwich was great and I got the low calorie turkey just to be safe 'cause with this diet I was being diligent and good.

But, then my friend insisted that I have part of her dessert as a reward for all the weight I'd lost. She reasoned, "Chocolate was a good for you food."

Well, it looked so chocolaty good my dedication thinned, I said, "Well, I guess I do deserve a little treat" and I dove right in and ate more than my share.

Then when I realized what I had done, I hung my head to hide my shame and walked quietly toward the door as I tried to avoid all the accusing stares.

The next day, I decided to go on crackers and water to make all that chocolate eating O.K.

But when I weighed at the end of the day, I weighed the same as I had the day before yesterday.

My friend told me that roughage was what I needed to kick my weight loss in gear, so I decided to eat carrot sticks and celery.

I stocked up on rabbit food at the grocery store, and I tried to nibble them all day but these foods are just not very tasty to me.

*Paula Jean Hight-Sullins*

But, since I had bought so much, I had to figure a way to eat it, and that's when I decided to use just a dab of ranch dressing to help me get it down.

And it helped immensely with the taste, and I began to really chow down and soon I began to smile instead of frown.

I could just eat rabbit food and cover it with ranch dressing, this diet was going to be a breeze.

When I got up the next morning feeling light as a feather, I eagerly stepped upon the scale and as I read the dial, I felt a buckle in my knees.

How could this be? Not only had I put back the three pounds that I had lost, but I had added an additional three.

Was this real or a nightmare? Pinch me and wake me up please. I can't believe it, it just can't be.

So I decide to fast for a day and instead of lunch, I walked around the block, not just one time but three!

It was a great idea and I really felt energized, I was so proud of me.

But when two o'clock rolled around, I felt my stomach roll and twinge.

So, I popped in some gum, but instead of quieting my hunger pain, my stomach began to growl and that's when I began to binge!

I grabbed my change purse and went to the machines in the hall.

I started dropping in quarters and dimes until I had no change left at all.

Then I sat there in the break room and started stuffing myself. I didn't care who saw or knew that I was a diet failure and disgrace.

And as the last piece of creamy milk chocolate was savored and swallowed, a sigh and blissful smile spread across my face.

I refused to weigh the next morning or the next and don't until this day,

'Cause I am pleasingly plump and I like it, so that is how I'm going to stay.

# Lord and Master

My cat thinks he's royalty and that's how he behaves.
In this house, he is the master and I am the slave.

He usually eats what I choose, but if he doesn't like it,
He'll turn with his nose and his tail in the air and sit.

Until, I pick up the old, get one he likes and change out the food.
Then he looks at me, takes a bite, then gobbles it down, he's so rude.

He likes to be petted while he sits in my lap and we watch T.V.
But if I laugh or move him, he digs his claws in my knee.

The Christmas tree, he thinks, is put up just for him.
He knocks the ornaments off and plays bat the ball with them.

If his litter box is not clean when it's time for his visit, he will not ask out
at the door.
Instead, he will leave me a nasty little present on the dining room floor.

If I put him outside and he doesn't want to go, he causes a commotion.
His growls, hisses, and hollers make me rethink my devotion.

But, when he looks up at me with those golden eyes and drops his chin,
I try to resist, but soon break down and let him back in.

He jumps in my lap as soon as I sit and rubs me with his head and gives
me Eskimo nose kisses and I give him hugs,
All of which I appreciate, but often wonder if while he was out, was he
rolling in the garbage or eating bugs?

And he is a sweet cat for awhile and then he reminds me again of my place.
He turns away abruptly and jumps down slapping me with his tail in
my face.

Yes, this totally spoiled and beloved cat has me trained very well.
I'm the servant and he's Lord and Master as everyone can tell.

For Midnight

# What a Beauty

Fwet Fwwwwwu! What a beauty!

Now that's what I call "sheer delight".

She is sooooo fine.

I cannot wait to take her out tonight.

Delectable and delicious,

Gorgeous curves, delectable design

Mmmmm . . . luscious, lipstick red

The glossy, highly polished kind.

She's all that's ever on my mind!

She's definitely one of a kind.

She's a page right out of a magazine.

She's the only one with whom I want to be seen.

For her, I have a deep abiding love.

Truly my six cylinder, fuel injected carburetor is by far,

The 'best of the best' for a jazzy, little, red sports car!

# E-Mail Me Please!

When I was a young woman in my teens and twenties, I used to love to write letters to relatives and friends.
I would ponder over what I was going to say, how I would say it, what I would write first and how I would end.

I took pains with my penmanship so it would be legible and easily read.
I'd write about the doings in town, at school, in my family, and of the ideas in my head.

Then I would enjoy the walk to the neighborhood postal box to drop it in, and return home to happily await a reply with anticipation.
Then several days later the postman would deliver a letter which I would tear open with glee and read with great interest and gratification.

I would read and reread every word and laugh or cry at the news in the letter.
Then I'd write another to share the news with others and I'd add new things to it to make it better.

Well, that was then, and now is now. I no longer write letters with paper and pen, I text or get texted and email and get emailed.
Thank God for technology and that writing and waiting for letters, though charming and quaint, is a ship that has sailed.

Even my checks have been replaced by my debit card and nothing on postage stamps do I spend.
For I get my mail quickly and easily online through, email and that is the only mail I send.

And I instant message, too for an immediate chat.
I want to know instantly what is happening and things like that.

*Paula Jean Hight-Sullins*

Though I can still write letters, I really don't want to.
They are a lost art that there is really no need to do.

My PC and phone texts are the fastest thing and the old way of communicating is one for the snails.
But, I admit, I still practice my writing skills, just in case, all this technology fails!

# Prayer

Thank you Dear God, my omnipotent exalted father, for loving me.

Thank you for hearing me when I pray, no matter how feeble and incomplete my prayers may be.

Thank you for understanding and intervening when I in my human frailty make colossally stupid mistakes.

Thank you for being patient with me and gently guiding me no matter how long it takes.

Thank you for your beloved son, Jesus, who suffered and died to take away my sin.

Thank you for forgiving me when my human nature causes me to forget and sin again.

Thank you for caring for me and the whole human race.

Thank you for caring about the earth and the tragedies we face.

Thank you for showing me how to live.

Thank you for teaching me how to forgive.

Thank you, Jesus, for your unconditional love.

Thank you, God, my magnificent heavenly father above.

Amen

# Disciples?

Have you sowed good seeds today?

Were you kind to others along your way?

Did you walk that extra mile?

Did you make someone that was hurting smile?

Did you remove a stumbling block or become one?

Can you say you thought and behaved like God's only son?

Did you take part in the gossip mill that meets every day for lunch?

Did you yell or curse because someone cut you off in traffic when you were in a time crunch?

Do we live what we profess as Christians? We are disciples each and everyone.

Let's live our lives spreading the Good News of our Lord, God's only son.

Let's spend our minutes, hours, and days making the world a better one.

After all, isn't that just what the disciples and Jesus would have done?

# It's a Piece of Cake

Have you ever heard people say, "It's a piece of cake?"

Especially when they are selling a new amazing product with a free gift to take

So, I eagerly push to the head of the line as if awaiting something great

And, I must admit, it does look easy when they demonstrate

So, I always bite and whatever it is I have to buy

And I rush home with it anxious to give it a try

I know it will be easy, 'cause they said "it's a piece of cake"

I rip open the package and see the first hurdle I must make.

Now to follow the instructions, let's see, Chinese, French, Russian, Spanish, Dutch, finally English

So, after an hour of assembly and re-assembly, it is ready to try and I cross my fingers and make a wish.

I followed the instructions carefully one step at a time as was advised

But to my chagrin, the results never, and I do mean never, work or look the same as was advertised.

But I know that it just needs a little tweak, so I re-examine my construction and tighten each bolt and screw.

*Paula Jean Hight-Sullins*

I had a few extra screws and bolts left over, so maybe I missed putting in one or two.

Then, I re-read the instructions and check the diagram and I attempt its usage again but with the same results and there's nothing I can do.

I say in disgust, "Well that really was 'a piece of cake', yep, "as easy as 1, 2, 3"

Another, really easy, $39.95, failure for gullible me.

I guess, I'll trash it and that decision was 'as easy as pie'.

HMmmm . . . . pie! That reminds me I have a new recipe I think I'll try!

# The Head and Not the Tail

I've heard it said, "Be the head and not the tail."
So, I decided to unfurl and let myself fly full sail.

Leaving all the worries and care to God
Stepping out in faith on new paths to trod.

For He has given me dreams and abilities.
That I should use and not limit my possibilities.

I'll step out in faith, give it my all, and by His grace, I'll not fail.
For with His guidance, I'll take the lead and be the head and not the tail!

# Tell Me Why?

Why did you ignore me? Turn a blind eye and a deaf ear.

You saw that I was suffering, you knew I needed someone to listen to me and really hear.

How can you sit there every Sunday, so pious and true? It's so wrong.

How can you profess your dedication to God and show your faith in worship and song?

And you see me and know that I am suffering yet, you must not believe what you see,

For a word of comfort, a hug of understanding, a prayer on bended knee, would've really helped me.

Shouldn't you ask yourself what Jesus would have done if he were here?

Would he have turned away and not gotten involved as I sat with my tears?

No, Jesus would have been there with me through it all.

He would never let me faint with despair, stumble or fall.

He would never let me suffer through this pain alone without one word to say.

He is compassion and caring He is the example for Christians who follow His way.

So why did you ignore me? When I needed your Christian love?

Why did you ignore me, couldn't you feel and hear Jesus directing you from above?

Why did you turn a blind eye and deaf ear?

Was I not important, famous or rich enough for your Christian love to appear?

It was not easy to live with the devastation and pain,

But Jesus never left me and He helped me endure the fire and the rain.

Will I return your actions when it is your turn to endure hardship or pain?

No, for no blessings or treasure in Heaven or earth will it gain.

Because I have felt God's compassion, His love surrounds me, and He is always near.

I will follow His example and I will not ignore you, turn a blind eye or deaf ear.

# Shambles

My wedding ring diamonds sparkle like stars in the sky
As I gaze at them through my tears and I wonder, why?

Oh, why couldn't things have turned out right,
Where are you, now? I need you holding me tonight.

When did things go bad?
I think of all that we had.

I don't understand. Was it me or you?
Is there anything now that I can do?

You pledged your love and gave me this ring
I never thought that this was not the real thing.

I remember the roses in my wedding bouquet.
My heart, my life, was so full that day.

I was so happy all I could do was smile,
How could things go wrong in such a little while?

I'm not the jealous type, and I trusted you.
Those long nights you worked I still had no clue.

I'm so confused, I don't know what to do
My life is in shambles, because I'm losing you.

# Are You Prepared?

Pain, suffering, anger, rage
At any time, at any age

All kinds of misery can be found
Cancer, crime, disasters are all around

But, I'm healthy and young, you say, it won't happen to me
That's an easy to believe lie, though a truth to some, it may be

And honestly it does happen to people just like you, Are you prepared?
What will you do?
Will your insurance cover it, will your family and friends help and be
there for you?

Misery is not exactly free, it can have a high cost that includes job loss,
disability, and poverty.
It might even call for the ultimate sacrifice with the loss of life, so have
you prepared your family?

It is true that we all have baggage of some kind or another that we carry
every day,
So when dealing with others please remember this in what you do and
say

And be mindful and prepared for whatever lies in wait.
For you never know when misery will be standing at your gate.

*Paula Jean Hight-Sullins*

# Goodbye Old Friend

As all things eventually will, it is your time to go. I will miss seeing you, steadfast in your old familiar place. Your walls surrounded me and protected me through the tempest and the calm. From my middle school years through to my academic success, you were there, tall and white and strong.

Your wide columns supporting the porch roof, under which I would swing sleepily with my sweet cat babies. And, the Moon Vine and Morning Glories grew up your spires, while the Sword Plant stood it's silent spiky guard.

Under the Mimosa's shady branches I sat, on the cool St. Augustine, covered with pods and wispy pink and gold blossoms, flying in the breeze and lying on the ground about me.

The homemade swing under the old massive Pecan was a favorite place, fast or slow, high or low, while the wind blew my hair to and fro. I tried to touch the tree's top branch or watched as my sister practiced to be a daredevil trapeze artist.

There's my room, the green walls with my rainbow "P" painted there, my specially designed by Daddy "built-ins", and the often raked, multi-green shag carpet. It was really "hip".

The rosewood piano stands on the staircase wall where Sally Mae pounded out "Under the Double Eagle" to instruct me about the importance of practice.

In back of the screened in breezeway, were my Mom's Elephant Ears and strawberry patch. It looked so professional. She was so proud; we were so proud, and the homemade shortcake and whipped cream, had no equal.

And do you remember Poncho, the cart pony who came to live in the back yard as an answer to my sister's persistent prayers and wishes? She loved him even though she was allergic to horse hair. She would mount up wearing her denim skirt with the fringe on the hem, cowgirl shirt, boots and hat and ride him over the prairies of our huge back yard. He loved her, too. He bit me on the back!

The old garage and the tin shed, an eyesore to my Mom, but known to me as my playhouse and mountaintop. There I made mud pies, entertained, raised children, or climbed to sit and read and think and ponder.

Then, there was the basketball goal nailed securely to the garage, where I played many games of "HORSE" with my sister, and which I credit with our starting positions on the high school teams. Through the years you withstood, without a major identity crisis, my mother's whims, and my daddy's carpentry—a new wall, a new hall, a bathroom, a fireplace; up with one, down with another, redo or undo; flocked paper, velvet drapes, sconces; Spanish, Early American, Contemporary, French; you stood firm and didn't budge an inch.

And the Christmas's! OH, the lovely Christmas's! You were beautiful. Each year, more beautiful than the years before. Never loud nor brash, always appropriate, reverent and elegant. The smells and sounds of the season within your walls. Real Cedar! Cut down fresh, on the family trek each year to the farm. Hot chocolate, spiced tea, wine and cheese; turkey, dressing, candies, and cakes; candles, garlands, wreaths, gift wrapping, cards; and phone calls, and family and friends and fellowship and fun.

You were our home, our fortress against the storms of nature and life. A protector; our haven of rest and recuperation.

We grew up there; my sister, my parents, and me. And like all who grow up, we left home, but home did not leave us.

*Paula Jean Hight-Sullins*

So, goodbye old friend. As all things eventually will, it is your time to go. I will miss seeing you steadfast in your familiar place, but in my memories and my heart, you will always be there. To me you still stand, steadfast, tall, white and strong, as always, my home.

# Winter

# 60th

Cheers and hooray; joy and glee.
Happy sixtieth birthday to me.

My hemorrhoids itch.
My baggy eyelids twitch.

My eyelashes are thin,
Every night I drink a jigger of gin.

My flaky scalp is dry.
And I make no tears to cry.

I walk with an old wooden cane.
'Cause both of my knees are in pain.

My figure has bumps and sags.
My thighs look like saddlebags.

My doctor has prescribed a handful of pills that I must take.
At his advice, I exercise until something, bleeds, gets pulled or breaks.

I color my hair and put wrinkle cream on my face every night,
I wear lots of black and a girdle to keep my flabby skin tight.

I am determined to be the best sixty year old that I can be.
Uphill battle or not, until it turns me into, or gets the best of me.

# A Miracle Pill

I use Deep Heat and a cane
'Cause my knees are in pain

I cannot kneel or bend to tie my shoe
'Cause my back gets a catch in it when I do

I want to exercise to regain my healthy glow
But if I lift one leg, then down with the other I go

I'd like to travel to visit friends and places in my car
But my eyesight is so poor, I can't get very far.

And if I did, after driving for a few miles, I'd have to stop
'Cause I would forget where I was going and I'd have to wait for a cop

After the policeman drives me home 'cause the way, I forgot.
He'll ask if I'll be traveling again and I'll answer, "I surely think not."

Why can't they come up with a few miracle pills?
It's the 21st century! I shouldn't be having all these ills.

*Paula Jean Hight-Sullins*

# Geriatric Dating

I've heard it said that after sixty-five, dating is not always fun.
Especially if you depend on dating sites or friends to get one.

The men are either balding and rotund, or blind in one eye with a hearing aid and cane,
Or, an aging rock star with tight leather pants and a long white shaggy mane,

Or, a rich old geezer looking for a young show toy to feed his ego while he pays for it all,
Or, they're only after one thing and it ain't friendship or commitment, or a game of basketball.

After age sixty-five, and rightfully so I guess, dating places and rituals have changed in the dating game.
Dancing is usually painful and due to arthritis and bursitis pain, could render one lame.

Eating out can be hazardous 'cause most are on special diets which restrict the menu
For eating "a la cart" is Russian Roulette, it's true, for heart attack and death could ensue.

So, what does that leave for the date? Well, movies, for one.
You would think that would be perfect and lots of fun.

Well, it could be unless your evening pills kick in and, you're both snoring before the show is done.
So, if you, like me, are still gorgeous and feel young, you might try dating a much younger someone.

But if you do, beware 'cause the language and point of reference is definitely not the same.
And if you are not careful you will get dumped for embarrassing them by not understanding the game".

"Hit you up", doesn't mean to "hit you" and if you say, "He looks like Kojak", they might say, "Oh yeah, the dog that was possessed".
Oh, well, all this to say, as you already might have guessed, dating after sixty-five can really be quite a mess!

# Christmas Time

Light the candles and display the evergreens and decorations across the nation.
Everywhere relatives, friends, and neighbors exchange gifts and conversation.

Red bows, ornaments, and green boughs covered with twinkle lights,
No matter where you are, this holiday is filled with such beautiful sights.

Remembering the old; looking forward to the new.
It's a time of hope and happiness, not a time to feel blue.

Christmas is a glorious celebration of Jesus birth,
To give thanks for this gift from God to the earth.

So ring the bells, and decorate with bright colors, silver and gold.
Sing carols and rejoice with gladness as the Christmas story is told.

# Winter Sounds

White snowflakes, silver bells, and tinsel, add to the decorations of red and green.

Sounds of 'Silent Night' and 'Alleluia' fill the air as festive carolers stroll onto the scene.

Then Santa enters the room amid squeals of delight as young eyes light up and open wide,

On his back a bulging red velvet sack is seen as children wait anxiously for gifts from inside.

Each normally squirmy child sits still watching in anticipation and wonder without saying a word.

As Santa and his helpers begin to pass out their treats and a merry "Ho, Ho, Ho," is heard.

# The New Year

The old year is out and a new year has begun
We pray dear Lord for a really good one

Who knows what kind of things
This brand new year brings.

Will it be abundant, prosperous, or full of want?
Will I finally win the battle of the bulge that I've fought?

Will our health be good throughout the year,
Or, will we face medical battles, uncertainties and fear?

Will we return kindnesses today and tomorrow?
Will we find companionship, romance, or sorrow?

A new year, to do better, be better, and to make a fresh start
A new year to pitch in, help out, listen to and be true to our heart

What will happen this new year? The truth and joy is, that we do not know.

So happily, hopefully, and prayerfully, into 2013, we bravely go.

# His Mercy Endures Forever

The Lord is good. He fails us never.

His mercy, grace, and love endure forever.

Sometimes I feel so stupid and unworthy, especially when,

I seem to make the same mistakes over and over again.

There may be different circumstances, or the same, but they are the same mistakes.

Dear Lord, please continue to forgive me, and in order not to make these mistakes, I will do whatever it takes.

Sometimes I think I am doing better but, then, the Devil trips me and I fall into a hole

I fall even though I truly strive to live more like Jesus, for that is my goal.

However as the Bible states, the spirit is willing, but the flesh is weak.

I truly try not to, but it seems that before I know what is happening the same actions upon me sneak.

I am so grateful and thank you dear Lord that even if it is the umpteenth time, whenever I am down, you forgive me and lift me up.

I notice that the more I ask for your forgiveness and help, the shallower becomes the hole I have dug for myself, and again you deliver me from this bitter cup.

I thank you Lord that you are good and your mercy endures forever.

And no matter how often I stumble, I'll fall from your love and grace never.

So even when things are messed up and I'm confused and misunderstood,

You forgive me and help me get back on the track to making my earthly and heavenly life good.

# New Era, New Day

It's a new age and a new day

With new inventions and cures coming our way

What an exciting time to be alive

I can't wait to see what's coming to help us survive

New gizmos, gadgets, applications,

New protocol, procedures, and automation

I was born in the era of black and white TV

Now I'm watching colorful shows in 3D

Digital images and instant picture communication

Questions about the future peaks the imagination

I'm so glad to be alive and living this way

Here in a brand new era and a brand new day

# Be Ye Kind

The Lord said, "Be ye kind to one another."

So I try to treat everyone as a sister or brother

Jesus was always kind to those he met: a leper, a harlot, a thief.

Following his example is what Christian's should do; this is my belief.

And when someone does a kindness to you,

Accept graciously and pass it on to someone new,

For isn't that just exactly what Jesus would do?

# Thank You Dear God

Thank you dear God, my omnipotent, exalted father for loving me
Thank you for hearing me when I pray as feeble as my prayers may be

Thank you for intervening when I, in my human frailty, make a colossally stupid mistake.
Thank you for being patient with me and gently guiding me no matter how long it might take.

Thank you for your beloved son, Jesus, who suffered and died for my sins.
Thank you for forgiving me, when my human nature causes me to forget and sin again.

Thank you for caring for me and the whole human race.
Thank you for caring about the earth and the trials we face.

Thank you for showing me how to live.
Thank you for teaching me how to forgive.

Thank you, Jesus, for your constant unfaltering love.
Thank you, Heavenly Father, who reigns from Heaven above.

# Mary Hill's Passing

A shock to all that she was taken away
But we must all go home someday

Choir harmony will be weak for her rich alto we will miss
As well as the prayers she gave for choir practice to dismiss

And her spot on the pew will be empty today
Though her spirit will be seen and felt in many ways

She was wise in years and her actions and words told us so
Yet those years were kind and on her they never did show

Positive, dependable, kind, and capable was she
And in fellowship with other Christians she liked to be

She was a loyal church member; faithful and true
If anyone ever needed anything, she was the first to do

She supplied whatever was needed and more.
For this in Heaven her rewards are in store

A keen wit was her companion and she used it in many ways
To put someone at ease, to help someone who was hurting and make
brighter their days.

She was a leader, a worker, a member, a teacher, and friend
But most important of all, she was a Christian to the end.

# Dating for the Older Set

I am statuesque and round
And though I want to be thin,
At sixty it's very hard I've found.

Dating is quite sparse at this stage
Most men of equal years
Don't want someone the same age

And even though dating younger women leaves them broke and often
in tears
Turning to a real woman the same age is one of their manly fears.
For we are not a size 4 with firm breasts and derrieres

We have sags and bags
Droopy arms and ugly skin tags

However, for this age and stage in life, we look just right.
But without having surgery the men our age just won't bite

So I guess I'll try for gentlemen older than me
'Cause I'd be considered their younger trophy
But most of all, because they can barely hear or see.

*Paula Jean Hight-Sullins*

# Will You? Will I?

When I am dead and gone,
Will anyone remember my life's song?
Will anyone pick up the harmony and carry it along?

When I am dead and gone,
Will anyone remember me fondly and smile or cry?
Will anyone understand what my life stood for,
what I valued and why?

When I am dead and gone,
Will anyone thank God for what I have done or for just knowing me?
Will anyone be proud of my legacy?

When I am dead and gone,
Will anyone visit my grave because they respected me and miss me so
much that any connection with me is what they crave?
Will anyone bring flowers in appreciation and recognition of the years of
toil, dedication, and care I selflessly gave?

When I'm dead and gone,
Will I have died forgotten, forsaken and alone?
When I die . . . .
Will I?